THE THREAT OF
GUN CONTROL

THE THREAT OF GUN CONTROL

By
BOB LAMKIN

Publishers

T. S. DENISON & COMPANY, INC.

Minneapolis

Library of Congress Card Number: 72-88080

Printed in the United States of America
by The Brings Press

PREFACE

The only time I have ever been forced to defend myself with a gun was during World War II while serving as a gunner on a B24 bomber in the Eighth Air Force over Europe.

The B24's that we flew were armed with ten 50-caliber machine guns each capable of firing 850 rounds per minute. With all of this firepower, none of it was ever used to kill people on the ground. That was not the purpose of the machine guns. Their use was to prevent and particularly to discourage attacks from other planes. *They were not offensive weapons*.

The same may be said about the handgun in my house. It is not there to kill people. Its purpose is to protect and to deter.

No one in this country would think of proposing a law whereby a Baptist must become Catholic within eighteen months or propose that all Catholics must attend the Methodist church ten times a year. A law like that would make the disturbances now going on in Northern Ireland look like a Sunday school picnic. It would contradict totally everything that all of us stand for and all of us live for.

So it is with gun control. Control breeds more control. Restriction breeds more restrictions. Indeed, who is to tell us with absolute certainty that the law against carrying a handgun concealed is a good law? Sometimes I wonder.

Next Sunday morning as many of us who wish may go to any church of any denomination at any place we choose or we may stay at home if we want to. That right is guaranteed by the Constitution of the United States.

This same document assures me in the same terms that I may always keep a handgun in my house.

It is as simple as that.

ROBERT B. LAMKIN

Watson, Illinois
June 1972

CONTENTS

THE CONSTITUTION AND GUN CONTROL

"They were dead. A whole family. Gentle, kindly people, people I knew—murdered," was one eyewitness reaction to the scene of the multiple murder of a farm family. Truman Capote recorded Larry Hendricks' account along with the interviews of others involved in the tragedy to produce one of the all-time best sellers, *In Cold Blood*.

November 15, 1959, put a town in Kansas named Holcomb on the map. Early that Sunday morning, two paroled inmates of Kansas State Penitentiary invaded the home of Finney County's most prominent farmer. By the time a neighbor girl arrived at nine to accompany the Clutter family to church, all four persons in the house were dead and on their way to a kind of fame they never knew in life.

A cellmate who had once worked for River Valley Farm assured Dick Hickock that Herbert William Clutter was a rich man. Hickock planned through long prison months of the haul he would make from the man that was famous throughout Finney County for never carrying cash, for writing a check for a haircut. First he needed a man that would insure there would be "no witnesses," a man who could kill without mercy. This was supplied by a new cellmate, Perry Smith.

Smith was the one who thrust the knife in and across Mr. Clutter's throat. While the victim strained against the cords binding his hands and feet, Smith fired a shotgun into the dying man's face. Kenyon Clutter, a lanky, blonde six-footer, 15 years old, was also taken to the basement where his father lay in the widening circle of blood. Nancy, the 17-year-old lead in Holcomb High School's production of *Tom Sawyer* on Friday night, was bound in her own bed.

She was the only member of the family whose mouth was not taped with adhesive strips winding around and around the head. It was Nancy that Smith remembered as "really nice. A very pretty girl, not spoiled or anything." It was Nancy that Smith remembered pleading, "Oh, no! Oh, please. No! No! No! No! Don't. Oh, please don't. Please!"

Mrs. Clutter, also tied in her bed, was the last to have the shotgun thrust inches away from her widely staring eyes. After hearing the three shots and the soft cries of her daughter, the woman that had been an invalid for years must have welcomed the blast that ended her life.

10

Later Smith recalled that while he was moving upstairs from the basement where Hickock was tying Mr. Clutter, he heard a noise. "A creaking overhead. I stopped at the foot of the stairs leading to the second floor. It was dark, and I didn't dare use the flashlight. But I could tell there was someone there. At the top of the stairs, silhouetted against a window. A figure. Then it moved away."

"For all I knew," Smith continued, "maybe it was somebody with a gun."

But it wasn't. The Clutters owned no handguns.

In many areas of the country, gun control laws imperil the ability of the law-abiding American citizen to defend himself and his property. What is most distressing is that these very laws are unconstitutional.

Using the Constitution of the United States as the foundation stone of this land, laws requiring the registration or confiscation of guns simply will not stand.

Indeed, the Second Amendment to the Constitution, often referred to as Article II of the Bill of Rights, specifically gives Americans the "right to keep and bear arms," a right which, it further says, "shall not be infringed." Yet, in spite of the clear meaning of Article II, the right to keep and bear arms has been slowly but surely curtailed in the state legislatures and in the United States Congress. The effectiveness with which individual Americans can protect themselves, their families, homes, and businesses is ever diminishing. These same laws reduce the collective strength Americans have as a nation in time of war or insurrection. Neither should the hunter, the sportsman, and the gun collector, all of whom are threatened by gun legislation, be forgotten.

The United States Constitution, consisting of seven original articles and twenty-six subsequent amendments, the first ten of which have been referred to as the Bill of Rights, is a document whose language and intent are specific. The founding fathers, working diligently at the Constitutional Convention to draft this basis for American government, set forth certain goals for this nation in what they believed were no uncertain terms. They could not have predicted that the Courts would ignore the meaning of the original document as has occurred.

Many nations, including Great Britain, had no formal constitutions to which their citizens, or their colonists for that matter, could turn for protection. While documents like the Magna Charta set forth certain principles and rights to be incorporated into the overall law of the land, no subject could rebuke Parliament by saying that an enacted law was unconstitutional. There is nothing in English law comparable to the United States Constitution. However, as far back as 1689, an English Declaration of Rights, subsequently termed a Bill of Rights, came into being.

We the People

of the United States, in order to form a more perfect Union, establish Justice, insure domestic Tranquility, provide for the common defence, promote the general Welfare, and secure the Blessings of Liberty to ourselves and our Posterity, do ordain and establish this Constitution for the United States of America.

Article. I.

Section. 1. All legislative Powers herein granted shall be vested in a Congress of the United States, which shall consist of a Senate and House of Representatives.

Section. 2. The House of Representatives shall be composed of Members chosen every second Year by the People of the several States, and the Electors in each State shall have the Qualifications requisite for Electors of the most numerous Branch of the State Legislature.

No Person shall be a Representative who shall not have attained to the Age of twenty five Years, and been seven Years a Citizen of the United States, and who shall not, when elected, be an Inhabitant of that State in which he shall be chosen.

Representatives and direct Taxes shall be apportioned among the several States which may be included within this Union, according to their respective Numbers, which shall be determined by adding to the whole Number of free Persons, including those bound to Service for a Term of Years, and excluding Indians not taxed, three fifths of all other Persons. The actual Enumeration shall be made within three Years after the first Meeting of the Congress of the United States, and within every subsequent Term of ten Years, in such Manner as they shall by Law direct. The Number of Representatives shall not exceed one for every thirty Thousand, but each State shall have at Least one Representative; and until such enumeration shall be made, the State of New Hampshire shall be entitled to chuse three, Massachusetts eight, Rhode Island and Providence Plantations one, Connecticut five, New York six, New Jersey four, Pennsylvania eight, Delaware one, Maryland six, Virginia ten, North Carolina five, South Carolina five, and Georgia three.

When vacancies happen in the Representation from any State, the Executive Authority thereof shall issue Writs of Election to fill such Vacancies.

The House of Representatives shall chuse their Speaker and other Officers; and shall have the sole Power of Impeachment.

Section. 3. The Senate of the United States shall be composed of two Senators from each State, chosen by the Legislature thereof for six Years; and each Senator shall have one Vote.

Immediately after they shall be assembled in Consequence of the first Election, they shall be divided as equally as may be into three Classes. The Seats of the Senators of the first Class shall be vacated at the Expiration of the second Year, of the second Class at the Expiration of the fourth Year, and of the third Class at the Expiration of the sixth Year, so that one third may be chosen every second Year; and if Vacancies happen by Resignation, or otherwise, during the Recess of the Legislature of any State, the Executive thereof may make temporary Appointments until the next Meeting of the Legislature, which shall then fill such Vacancies.

No Person shall be a Senator who shall not have attained to the Age of thirty Years, and been nine Years a Citizen of the United States, and who shall not, when elected, be an Inhabitant of that State for which he shall be chosen.

The Vice President of the United States shall be President of the Senate, but shall have no Vote, unless they be equally divided.

The Senate shall chuse their other Officers, and also a President pro tempore, in the Absence of the Vice President, or when he shall exercise the Office of President of the United States.

The Senate shall have the sole Power to try all Impeachments. When sitting for that Purpose, they shall be on Oath or Affirmation. When the President of the United States is tried, the Chief Justice shall preside: And no Person shall be convicted without the Concurrence of two thirds of the Members present.

Judgment in Cases of Impeachment shall not extend further than to removal from Office, and disqualification to hold and enjoy any Office of honor, Trust or Profit under the United States: but the Party convicted shall nevertheless be liable and subject to Indictment, Trial, Judgment and Punishment, according to Law.

Section. 4. The Times, Places and Manner of holding Elections for Senators and Representatives, shall be prescribed in each State by the Legislature thereof; but the Congress may at any time by Law make or alter such Regulations, except as to the Places of chusing Senators.

The Congress shall assemble at least once in every Year, and such Meeting shall be on the first Monday in December, unless they shall by Law appoint a different Day.

Section. 5. Each House shall be the Judge of the Elections, Returns and Qualifications of its own Members, and a Majority of each shall constitute a Quorum to do Business; but a smaller Number may adjourn from day to day, and may be authorized to compel the Attendance of absent Members, in such Manner, and under such Penalties as each House may provide.

Each House may determine the Rules of its Proceedings, punish its Members for disorderly Behaviour, and, with the Concurrence of two thirds, expel a Member.

Each House shall keep a Journal of its Proceedings, and from time to time publish the same, excepting such Parts as may in their Judgment require Secrecy; and the Yeas and Nays of the Members of either House on any question shall, at the Desire of one fifth of those Present, be entered on the Journal.

Neither House, during the Session of Congress, shall, without the Consent of the other, adjourn for more than three days, nor to any other Place than that in which the two Houses shall be sitting.

Section. 6. The Senators and Representatives shall receive a Compensation for their Services, to be ascertained by Law, and paid out of the Treasury of the United States. They shall in all Cases, except Treason, Felony and Breach of the Peace, be privileged from Arrest during their Attendance at the Session of their respective Houses, and in going to and returning from the same; and for any Speech or Debate in either House, they shall not be questioned in any other Place.

No Senator or Representative shall, during the Time for which he was elected, be appointed to any civil Office under the Authority of the United States, which shall have been created, or the Emoluments whereof shall have been encreased during such time; and no Person holding any Office under the United States, shall be a Member of either House during his Continuance in Office.

Section. 7. All Bills for raising Revenue shall originate in the House of Representatives; but the Senate may propose or concur with Amendments as on other Bills.

Every Bill which shall have passed the House of Representatives and the Senate, shall, before it become a Law, be presented to the President of the

Congrefs OF THE

begun and held at the City

Wednesday the fourth of March, one thou

THE Conventions of a number of the States, ha

or abuse of its powers, that further declaratory and restrictive clauses should be added: And as extending

RESOLVED by the Senate and House

concurring that the following Articles be proposed to the Legislatures of the several States, as amendments

said Legislatures, to be valid to all intents and purposes, as part of the said Constitution; viz.ᵗ

ARTICLES in addition to, and amendmen

of the several States, pursuant to the fifth Article of the original Constitution.

Article the first..... After the first enumeration required by the first Article of the Constitution, there shall b

which, the proportion shall be so regulated by Congrefs, that there shall be not lef

until the number of Representatives shall amount to two hundred, after which the

nor more than one Representative for every fifty thousand persons.

Article the second... No law, varying the compensation for the services of the Senators and Representatives,

Article the third...... Congrefs shall make no law respecting an establishment of religion, or prohibiting the fr

afsemble, and to petition the Government for a redrefs of grievances

Article the fourth.... A well regulated militia, being necefsary to the security of a free State, the right

14

United States

of New-York, on

sand seven hundred and eighty nine

ing at the time of their adopting the Constitution, expressed a desire, in order to prevent misconstruction

the ground of public confidence in the Government, will best ensure the beneficent ends of its institution

of Representatives of the United States of America, in Congress assembled, two thirds of both Houses

to the Constitution of the United States, all, or any of which Articles, when ratified by three fourths of the

d of the Constitution of the United States of America, proposed by Congress, and ratified by the Legislatures

one Representative for every thirty thousand, until the number shall amount to one hundred, after

than one hundred Representatives, nor less than one Representative for every forty thousand persons,

roportion shall be so regulated by Congress, that there shall not be less than two hundred Representatives,

hall take effect, until an election of Representatives shall have intervened.

exercise thereof; or abridging the freedom of speech, or of the press, or the right of the people peaceably to

f the people to keep and bear arms, shall not be infringed.

As early as 1066, English landowners were required to maintain arms in defense of the nation and the King. There were no formal organized armies, but only *milites,* or militias of the people. After some political and social turmoil, a Convention Parliament met in January of 1689, and declared a vacancy of the throne. William and Mary were proclaimed King and Queen only after they agreed to accept a Declaration of Rights presented to them on February 12th of that year. The Declaration claimed to contain the "true, ancient, and indubitable rights of the people," the rights we might call *natural* today. The maintenance of a standing army in time of peace was declared illegal, but a provision allowing the subjects to "have arms for their defense" was incorporated.

Our own Bill of Rights has its roots in this tradition. During the constitutional debates on ratification of the original document by the states, the issue of a bill of rights arose. Many delegates, expressing the wishes of their respective states, urged the Philadelphia convention to include such a bill within the framework of the constitution. The document had already been framed after much agonizing debate, and it was decided instead to incorporate these declarations of rights as Amendments to the Constitution. Twelve such Amendments were subsequently submitted to the states for ratification and ten selected. These first ten Amendments to the Constitution came to be known as the Bill of Rights.

Signing of the Declaration of Independence marked the beginnings of independence and liberty for all Americans, including the Article II Bill of Rights provision guaranteeing the right to bear arms.

The right to bear arms is deeply entrenched in the proposals of many states to the Constitutional Convention. Samuel Adams, a scholarly Massachusetts leader, had introduced in his state convention a proposal that the "Constitution never construed to authorise Congress to prevent the people of the United States, who are peaceable citizens from keeping their own arms."

New Hampshire, the ninth state to ratify, proposed an Amendment which stated clearly that "Congress shall never disarm any citizen unless such are or have been in actual rebellion."

Rhode Island simply said that "the people have a right to keep and bear arms" while a Pennsylvania provision enumerated the right of the people to bear arms in their own defense, defense of their state, or the United States, and for killing game. It went on to say that "no law shall be enacted for disarming the people except for crimes committed or in a real case of public injury from individuals." Standing armies were discouraged and a definite subordination of the military to the civilian power was established. This relationship was one which was shared by nearly all the states whose delegates were assembled in Philadelphia.

James Madison, often referred to as "the father of the Constitution" was as instrumental as any of the delegates in including the right to bear arms among the many rights enumerated in the first ten Amendments. He assembled, digested, and reworked

James Madison, father of the United States Constitution, and firm believer in the right of the people to keep and bear arms.

the many proposals from the various states, each aimed at preserving the right to bear arms.

In Madison's own state of Virginia, a strong Bill of Rights had already been written. The right to bear arms, the subordination of military to civilian power, the protection against quartering of soldiers in one's home, in time of peace, against the will of the home-owner, and provisions for state militias in contrast to national armies in times of peace were among the proposals sent to the Constitutional Convention. North Carolina looked upon Virginia's model as ideal and submitted an identical amendment.

The delegates and the citizens they represented remembered only too well that they had once been colonists, that the British had quartered themselves in the colonists' homes, that they had used the colonists' own weapons against them.

It was back in 1775 that British General Gage dispatched seven hundred troops to seize the munitions and supplies of the "patriots" and the Minute Men Militia. But it was the militia, pouring in from all sides, that led Gage to retreat from Lexington and Concord with three times the number of American casualties.

As a result, the Virginia Bill of Rights, with its provision for the right to bear arms became a major thrust at the Convention. In fact, every single provision of the Virginia Bill of Rights, except one allowing conscientious objectors to avoid bearing arms by finding suitable replacements, found its way into the Bill of Rights of the United States Constitution. The inherent right of the people to keep and bear arms became the Second Amendment.

So *natural* was this right, existing long before the Founding Fathers met to draft the Constitution, Jefferson used it as the basic argument in favor of the Revolution against England. The Continental Congress had adopted a resolution condemning King George III for his tyrannical policies. Titled the "Declaration of the Causes and Necessity of Taking Up Arms," it was precursor of the Declaration of Independence.

A regular standing army, like the one we know today, did not exist in colonial times. The main means of protection was individually armed citizens, members of local militias. When Jefferson spoke, therefore, of the necessity of taking up arms, he spoke of the necessity of the individual citizens— then only colonists—to take up arms to protect themselves against the tyrannies of foreign power.

Thomas Jefferson said that "whenever any form of government becomes destructive of these ends," referring to man's natural rights, "it is the right of the people to alter or abolish it . . ." He was clearly speaking of revolution, the kind of armed overthrow which led the colonies to independence in the Revolutionary War.

"What country can preserve its liberties if its rulers are not warned from time to time that its people preserve the spirit of resistance? Let them

Thomas Jefferson, draftsman of the Declaration justifying the American Revolution in pursuit of freedom for Americans.

take arms," Jefferson said a decade later. Americans do not often think in terms of invasions or tyrannical government in this day and age, but they should not forget the lessons of the Hungarian Revolution in 1956, the Cuban change of government, or the Nazi invasions of Europe during World War II. A well-armed citizenry could have been instrumental in each case in supplying that "resistance" Thomas Jefferson spoke of.

The founding fathers of the United States Constitution incorporated into Article II of the Bill of Rights both the natural right of the individual to protect himself, i.e., to keep and bear arms, and the right of a well-regulated militia in defense of the nation. The Virginia Declaration of Rights, first adopted on June 12, 1776, stated, for example, that "a well-regulated militia, composed of the body of the people, trained to arms, is the proper, natural, and safe defense of a free state."

The Federal Bill of Rights, proclaimed December 15, 1791, stated that "a well-regulated Militia being necessary to the security of a free State, the right of the people to keep and bear Arms shall not be infringed." Some source of confusion originates in the reference to the Militia. It must be remembered, however, that back in the 1700s, the militia was in fact the body of the people. Every able-bodied man for all intents and purposes, was part of the militia. A standing army as we know it today did not exist. Groups of individual citizens protected the interests of the individual communities and of the State; hence, the "right of the People" to keep and bear arms must be an individual as well as a collective right. Many contemporary writers and historians discount Article II of the Bill of Rights as "obsolete" or "dead" today. They simply say it has no practical applications.

William O. Douglas, Supreme Court Justice, for example, said in a recent book, *A Living Bill of Rights*, that the "twentieth century citizen is apt to be much less concerned about the right of the people to bear arms that is secured by the Second Amendment" than about other guarantees of free speech, press, and assembly which derive from the First Amendment. While some citizens may be more concerned with other rights, the right to bear arms is very much an important issue in the twentieth century, just as it was when America was founded.

As far back as 1875, the United States Supreme Court considered the issue of this right. In *U. S. v. Cruikshank*, the Court struck down prosecution for interference with the right to bear arms on the ground that this right existed long before the United States Constitution was written. The right, the Court said, was not "granted or secured" by the Federal Constitution or by law. The Bill of Rights, it was argued, merely stated that the government could not interfere with these self-evident natural rights of man. It has been argued that this decision is faulty because while the Constitution could not grant the right to bear arms, something which already existed prior to its inception, it could certainly "secure" this right in the sense of "make secure." This meaning of the word is the same as is used in the Preamble to the Constitution and the Declaration of Independence.

To insure, too, that these natural rights were not infringed, the various states of the union in their own constitutions included provisions of the right to bear arms.

In Alaska, Georgia, Hawaii, Louisiana, North Carolina, Rhode Island and South Carolina, the individual constitutions guarantee that this right is not to be infringed.

The constitutions of Arkansas, Maryland and Tennessee declare that citizens have the right to bear arms for common defense. In Massachusetts, the state constitution refers to the "people" rather than "citizens."

Citizens are guaranteed the right to bear arms in defense of the state in Alabama, Arizona, Connecti- -cut, Kentucky, Michigan, Pennsylvania, South Dakota, Texas, Washington and Wyoming, by their constitutions. The people of Florida, Indiana, Oregon and Vermont are granted the same rights in slightly different language.

The question of a citizen's right to bear arms in defense of himself is well settled in the state constitutions of Alabama, Arizona, Connecticut, Kentucky, Mississippi, Missouri, New Mexico, Oklahoma, Penn-

CONSTITUTION OF KENTUCKY

PREAMBLE

We, the people of the Commonwealth of Kentucky, grateful to Almighty God for the civil, political and religious liberties we enjoy, and invoking the continuance of these blessings, do ordain and establish this Constitution.

BILL OF RIGHTS

That the great and essential principles of liberty and free government may be recognized and established, we declare that:

§ 1. **Rights of life, liberty, worship, pursuit of safety and happiness, free speech, acquiring and protecting property, peaceable assembly, redress of grievances, bearing arms.** All men are, by nature, free and equal, and have certain inherent and inalienable rights, among which may be reckoned:

First: The right of enjoying and defending their lives and liberties.

Second: The right of worshipping Almighty God according to the dictates of their consciences.

Third: The right of seeking and pursuing their safety and happiness.

Fourth: The right of freely communicating their thoughts and opinions.

Fifth: The right of acquiring and protecting property.

Sixth: The right of assembling together in a peaceable manner for their common good, and of applying to those invested with the power of government for redress of grievances or other proper purposes, by petition, address or remonstrance.

Seventh: The right to bear arms in defense of themselves and of the State, subject to the power of the General Assembly to enact laws to prevent persons from carrying concealed weapons.

sylvania, South Dakota, Texas, Washington and Wyoming, each of which guarantees this right to "every citizen."

Mississippi, Oklahoma and Missouri have specific constitutional provisions which declare that the right of the citizen to bear arms in defense of his property shall never be questioned.

Since each of these states used the Federal Constitution as a model, a large number of legislators must have interpreted the United States Constitution's Second Amendment to *mean what it says*—the right of the people to keep and bear arms shall not be infringed.

Several states have constitutions which do not specifically afford any right in connection with arms, probably because their legislators believed that these rights were guaranteed by the Federal Constitution. Since the United States Constitution is the constitution of *all* Americans, it is not necessary that individual state constitutions repeat the provisions of the Federal model.

In New York, the constitution says nothing about the right to bear arms, but the state has gone one step further. The Sullivan Law actually takes away from the people the basic right to bear arms guaranteed by the United States Constitution. Of course, this cannot be done constitutionally, but the courts have never really tackled the basic issue of the Second Amendment to the Constitution.

The Supreme Court has upheld certain national firearm laws, but it has consistently skirted the issue of Article II of the Bill of Rights. In 1894, for example, the case of *Miller v. Texas* came to rest in the hands of the Supreme Court justices. A Texas statute prohibiting the carrying of dangerous weapons by the individual was said not to violate the Second Amendment, since the restrictions of this amendment have effect, the Court ruled, "only upon the Federal power, and have no reference to proceedings in the state courts."

In 1939, in *United States v. Miller*, the Court ruled that the Second Amendment did not protect an individual who shipped an unregistered firearm in violation of the National Firearms Act. A lower court had previously dismissed an indictment under this Act, but the Supreme Court subsequently reversed the decision. It held that unless the defendant was able to show that the weapon in question related to a well-regulated militia, the Second Amendment could not apply.

The United States Supreme Court has never confronted directly the issue of the Second Amendment's meaning. It has been skirted repeatedly. A number of Justices, however, in their activities on and off the bench, seem to indicate general agreement with the contention that the Courts often go too far in bending the meaning of this original document of American law. Justice Douglas, for example, stated in the New York University Law Review

(Volume 38), referring to the Constitution, that "The closest the framers came to the affirmative side of liberty was in the right to bear arms. Yet this too has been greatly modified by judicial construction."

The former Chief Justice of the Supreme Court, Earl Warren, was not known for his strict Constitutionalist approach to law; indeed, he was often termed a "liberal" by those who favored a stricter application of the original principles set down in the United States Constitution. It is interesting to note, however, that when he presided over the Warren Commission—the body which sifted through tons of data on the assassination of President Kennedy—no recommendations on antigun legislation were made. This contrasted sharply with later Presidential commissions formed to examine violence in the cities. Some of these recommended strong gun-control measures, neither aware of their obvious ineffectiveness in combatting crime nor the unconstitutional nature of the proposed laws.

Under our judicial system, the Supreme Court cannot just offer advice or opinions, except when a case or controversy is brought before it through legal channels. Such challenges to laws usually take many years, moving up from lower courts where appeal after appeal must be filed.

Back in 1793, as an example, President Washington asked the Supreme Court to render an opinion on the meaning of certain treaties. John Jay, then Chief Justice of the High Court, told the President the

Court was powerless to give such judgments and therefore would not.

More often than not, even when a major case reaches the Court, interpretation might hinge on one of very many facets of a law, and if a defendant's plea is upheld, it may be more on the basis of a technicality than the overall spirit of the law. New York's Sullivan Law, for example, literally has hundreds of provisions, having been amended over and over again. If a man files suit against the law as an abridgment of certain rights, perhaps the Second Amendment right to bear arms, the Court may very well disallow some small portion of that law for some very technical reason. But no decision as to the overall Constitutionality of the law in relation to the Second Amendment has yet been made.

GUN CONTROL LEGISLATION

Gun control legislation has many failings. The most important, of course, is the failure of gun laws to meet the requirements of the Constitution of the United States. Since the Second Amendment clearly establishes that the right to keep arms "shall not be infringed," laws regulating guns by registration or confiscation are inherently unconstitutional.

Other parts of the Constitution, however, afford equally valid protection against gun control. The Fifth Amendment, for example, states that "No person . . . shall be compelled in any criminal case to be a witness against himself. . . ." Obviously, firearms registration requirements might compel a person who unlawfully possesses a firearm to admit the unlawful possession, in effect testifying against himself. On January 30, 1968, the United States Supreme Court, in the landmark decision of *Haynes v. United States*, stated that a proper Fifth Amendment claim provides a defense to prosecution either for failure to register a firearm or for possession of an unregistered gun under the National Firearms Act. In effect, the court ruled that the major requirements of this act were unconstitutional.

The Fourteenth Amendment, which became part of the U. S. Constitution in 1868, stated, "No State shall make or enforce any law which shall abridge the privileges or immunities of citizens of the United States; nor shall any State deprive any person of life, liberty, or property, without due process of law. . . ." Therefore, if the Second Amendment guarantees a certain privilege to the individual—the right to keep and bear arms—state-wide gun laws such as New York's notorious Sullivan Law are patently unconstitutional.

We can challenge gun control attempts on Constitutional grounds, but we can with equal ease see that for pragmatic reasons these same laws are worthless. They simply aren't effective in doing what they are designed to do—curb crime.

Let us compare several states. New York affords no protection to the law-abiding citizen regarding the right to own a handgun; it is strictly controlled under the Sullivan Law. A number of other states' constitutions specifically provide for gun ownership by the individual citizen.

The Montana Constitution, like those of Colorado and Mississippi, states that "The right of any person to keep or bear arms in defense of his own home, person, and property, or in aid of the civil power when thereto legally summoned, shall not be called in question."

The Constitution of the State of Pennsylvania says in like fashion that "The right of the citizens to bear arms in defense of themselves and the state shall not be questioned."

If we were to believe gun-control-law proponents, we'd expect Montana and Pennsylvania to have crime rates in excess of those in New York where gun control is rigid and strict. An examination of the Federal Bureau of Investigation statistics for 1970 will tell the story. In the classification of murder and nonnegligent manslaughter, New York showed a rate of 7.9 per 100,000 population. Pennsylvania was shown at 5.3 and Montana at 3.2, less than half New York's level. In robberies, New York showed the astronomical level of 443.3, the highest figure in the nation. Pennsylvania had 88.4 and Montana 22.2. Those states which do not interfere with the individual's right to keep and bear arms *do not* have higher crime rates than those which restrict the law-abiding citizen. They are, on the contrary, significantly lower.

Gun control legislation is not something new on either the national or local level. As early as 1795, Massachusetts enacted a law prohibiting the carrying of "offensive weapons" in public. In Kentucky, some years later, a law provided that concealed pistols were not to be worn, except when traveling. The back country of Kentucky was every bit as danger-

Index of Crime by State, 1970

Area	Population	Total Crime Index	Violent[1] crime	Property[2] crime	Murder and nonnegligent manslaughter	Forcible rape	Robbery	Aggravated assault	Burglary	Larceny $50 and over	Auto theft
MONTANA											
Standard Metropolitan Statistical Area	169,171										
Area actually reporting	100.0%	4,442	279	4,163	4	22	85	168	1,629	1,859	675
Other cities	202,343										
Area actually reporting	94.9%	3,466	164	3,302	7	10	35	112	1,076	1,730	496
Estimated total	100.0%	3,654	173	3,481	7	11	37	118	1,134	1,824	523
Rural	322,895										
Area actually reporting	87.7%	2,869	283	2,586	10	35	29	209	1,193	1,093	300
Estimated total	100.0%	3,270	322	2,948	11	40	33	238	1,360	1,246	342
State total	694,409	11,366	774	10,592	22	73	155	524	4,123	4,929	1,540
Rate per 100,000 inhabitants		1,636.8	111.5	1,525.3	3.2	10.5	22.3	75.5	593.7	709.8	221.8
NEBRASKA											
Standard Metropolitan Statistical Area	635,571										
Area actually reporting	97.9%	15,913	2,378	13,535	35	97	809	1,437	4,931	4,863	3,741
Estimated total	100.0%	16,042	2,384	13,658	35	97	810	1,442	4,979	4,923	3,756
Other cities	316,440										
Area actually reporting	94.3%	3,298	173	3,125	5	23	23	122	1,175	1,589	361
Estimated total	100.0%	3,496	182	3,314	5	24	24	129	1,246	1,685	383
Rural	531,780										
Area actually reporting	68.7%	2,045	114	1,931	3	12	11	88	867	932	132
Estimated total	100.0%	2,974	165	2,809	4	17	16	128	1,261	1,356	192
State total	1,483,791	22,512	2,731	19,781	44	138	850	1,699	7,486	7,964	4,331
Rate per 100,000 inhabitants		1,517.2	184.1	1,333.1	3.0	9.3	57.3	114.5	504.5	536.7	291.9

NEVADA

	Population	Total	(violent)	(property)	(murder)	(rape)	(robbery)	(agg. assault)	(burglary)	(larceny)	(auto theft)
Standard Metropolitan Statistical Area	394,356										
Area actually reporting	93.9%	16,115	1,557	14,558	32	81	806	638	6,992	4,815	2,751
Estimated total	100.0%	17,416	1,675	15,741	34	88	863	690	7,498	5,296	2,947
Other cities	37,189										
Area actually reporting	100.0%	681	63	618	2	---	12	49	212	314	92
Rural	57,193										
Area actually reporting	89.4%	1,281	187	1,094	6	7	41	133	363	561	170
Estimated total	100.0%	1,434	210	1,224	7	8	46	149	406	628	190
State total	**488,738**	**19,531**	**1,948**	**17,583**	**43**	**96**	**921**	**888**	**8,116**	**6,238**	**3,229**
Rate per 100,000 inhabitants		3,996.2	398.6	3,597.6	8.8	19.6	188.4	181.7	1,660.6	1,276.3	660.7

NEW HAMPSHIRE

	Population	Total	(violent)	(property)	(murder)	(rape)	(robbery)	(agg. assault)	(burglary)	(larceny)	(auto theft)
Standard Metropolitan Statistical Area	223,941										
Area actually reporting	95.2%	2,207	122	2,085	7	6	35	74	916	788	381
Estimated total	100.0%	2,309	129	2,180	8	6	36	79	958	817	405
Other cities	308,990										
Area actually reporting	92.9%	4,363	196	4,167	1	19	41	135	1,897	1,701	569
Estimated total	100.0%	4,694	210	4,484	1	20	44	145	2,041	1,831	612
Rural	204,750										
Area actually reporting	100.0%	1,795	74	1,721	6	18	9	41	1,173	296	262
State total	**737,681**	**8,798**	**413**	**8,385**	**15**	**44**	**89**	**265**	**4,172**	**2,944**	**1,269**
Rate per 100,000 inhabitants		1,192.7	56.0	1,136.7	2.0	6.0	12.1	35.9	566.6	399.1	172.0

NEW JERSEY

	Population	Total	(violent)	(property)	(murder)	(rape)	(robbery)	(agg. assault)	(burglary)	(larceny)	(auto theft)
Standard Metropolitan Statistical Area	5,511,330										
Area actually reporting	100.0%	156,656	18,170	141,486	364	760	10,977	6,069	59,979	46,458	35,049
Other cities	1,496,566										
Area actually reporting	100.0%	33,837	2,268	31,569	37	143	1,119	969	12,961	13,983	4,625
Rural	160,268										
Area actually reporting	100.0%	3,216	145	3,071	11	24	49	61	1,709	1,079	283
State total	**7,168,164**	**196,709**	**20,583**	**176,126**	**412**	**927**	**12,145**	**7,099**	**74,649**	**61,520**	**39,957**
Rate per 100,000 inhabitants		2,744.2	287.1	2,457.1	5.7	12.9	169.4	99.0	1,041.4	858.2	557.4

See footnotes at end of table.

35

Index of Crime by State, 1970

Area	Population	Total Crime Index	Violent[1] crime	Property[2] crime	Murder and non-negligent man-slaughter	Forci-ble rape	Robbery	Aggra-vated assault	Burglary	Larceny $50 and over	Auto theft
NEW MEXICO											
Standard Metropolitan Statistical Area	315,774										
Area actually reporting	100.0%	15,300	1,622	13,678	23	124	465	1,010	6,257	5,222	2,199
Other cities	385,017										
Area actually reporting	96.2%	10,597	908	9,689	23	48	165	672	4,262	4,468	959
Estimated total	100.0%	11,020	945	10,075	24	50	172	699	4,432	4,646	997
Rural	315,209										
Area actually reporting	98.3%	2,746	400	2,346	47	45	34	274	894	678	774
Estimated total	100.0%	2,793	408	2,385	48	46	35	279	909	689	787
State total	1,016,000	29,113	2,975	26,138	95	220	672	1,988	11,598	10,557	3,983
Rate per 100,000 inhabitants		2,865.5	292.8	2,572.6	9.4	21.7	66.1	195.7	1,141.5	1,039.1	392.0
NEW YORK											
Standard Metropolitan Statistical Area	15,726,064										
Area actually reporting	99.2%	680,259	120,479	559,780	1,361	2,685	80,133	36,300	241,070	197,613	121,097
Estimated total	100.0%	682,690	120,650	562,040	1,364	2,691	80,213	36,382	241,921	198,664	121,455
Other cities	950,184										
Area actually reporting	93.3%	13,396	1,243	12,153	20	37	263	923	5,305	5,567	1,281
Estimated total	100.0%	14,357	1,332	13,025	21	40	282	989	5,686	5,966	1,373
Rural	1,514,492										
Area actually reporting	100.0%	16,406	994	15,412	54	92	146	702	9,655	4,493	1,264
State total	18,190,740	713,453	122,976	590,477	1,439	2,823	80,641	38,073	257,262	209,123	124,092
Rate per 100,000 inhabitants		3,922.1	676.0	3,246.0	7.9	15.5	443.3	209.3	1,414.2	1,149.6	682.2

NORTH CAROLINA

Standard Metropolitan Statistical Area...	1,896,423	51,327	8,415	42,912	250	268	1,693	6,204	20,057	18,354	4,501
Area actually reporting	90.0%										
Estimated total	100.0%	54,143	8,771	45,372	266	289	1,758	6,458	21,343	19,359	4,670
Other cities	862,148	16,867	3,592	13,275	85	103	348	3,056	5,577	6,122	1,576
Area actually reporting	85.0%										
Estimated total	100.0%	19,842	4,225	15,617	100	121	409	3,595	6,561	7,202	1,854
Rural	2,323,488	8,501	2,238	6,263	82	95	138	1,923	3,344	2,453	466
Area actually reporting	41.2%										
Estimated total	100.0%	20,611	5,427	15,184	199	230	335	4,663	8,107	5,948	1,129
State total	**5,082,059**	**94,596**	**18,423**	**76,173**	**565**	**640**	**2,502**	**14,716**	**36,011**	**32,509**	**7,653**
Rate per 100,000 inhabitants		1,861.4	362.5	1,498.9	11.1	12.6	49.2	289.6	708.6	639.7	150.6

NORTH DAKOTA

Standard Metropolitan Statistical Area..	73,653	1,041	31	1,010	2	6	9	14	240	652	118
Area actually reporting	100.0%										
Estimated total	100.0%										
Other cities	189,756	2,583	63	2,520		11	15	37	773	1,435	312
Area actually reporting	100.0%										
Estimated total	100.0%										
Rural	354,352	1,311	96	1,215	1	17	13	65	618	489	108
Area actually reporting	81.8%										
Estimated total	100.0%	1,603	117	1,486	1	21	16	79	756	598	132
State total	**617,761**	**5,227**	**211**	**5,016**	**3**	**38**	**40**	**130**	**1,769**	**2,685**	**562**
Rate per 100,000 inhabitants		846.1	34.2	812.0	.5	6.2	6.5	21.0	286.4	434.6	91.0

OHIO

Standard Metropolitan Statistical Area..	8,272,512	219,811	27,152	192,659	656	1,554	14,974	9,968	76,265	67,005	49,389
Area actually reporting	96.0%										
Estimated total	100.0%	224,535	27,546	196,989	664	1,582	15,096	10,204	78,075	68,773	50,141
Other cities	987,718	13,876	1,513	12,363	13	59	299	1,142	5,602	5,319	1,442
Area actually reporting	89.6%										
Estimated total	100.0%	15,480	1,689	13,791	15	66	334	1,274	6,249	5,933	1,609
Rural	1,391,787	9,169	728	8,441	14	36	76	602	4,625	3,301	515
Area actually reporting	69.8%										
Estimated total	100.0%	13,143	1,044	12,099	20	52	109	863	6,629	4,732	738
State total	**10,652,017**	**253,158**	**30,279**	**222,879**	**699**	**1,700**	**15,539**	**12,341**	**90,953**	**79,438**	**52,488**
Rate per 100,000 inhabitants.		2,376.6	284.3	2,092.4	6.6	16.0	145.9	115.9	853.9	745.8	492.8

See footnotes at end of table.

Index of Crime by State, 1970

Area	Population	Total Crime Index	Violent crime [1]	Property crime [2]	Murder and non-negligent manslaughter	Forcible rape	Robbery	Aggravated assault	Burglary	Larceny $50 and over	Auto theft
OKLAHOMA											
Standard Metropolitan Statistical Area											
Area actually reporting	1,280,531	34,632	3,473	31,159	94	292	1,154	1,933	14,533	10,976	5,650
	99.8%										
Estimated total	100.0%	34,686	3,477	31,209	94	292	1,155	1,936	14,553	11,001	5,655
Other cities	566,885										
Area actually reporting	87.7%	7,940	655	7,285	14	29	98	514	2,875	3,620	790
Estimated total	100.0%	9,053	747	8,306	16	33	112	586	3,278	4,127	901
Rural	711,837										
Area actually reporting	63.1%	3,906	528	3,378	26	47	70	385	1,560	1,507	311
Estimated total	100.0%	6,190	837	5,353	41	75	111	610	2,472	2,388	493
State total	2,559,253	49,929	5,061	44,868	151	400	1,378	3,132	20,303	17,516	7,049
Rate per 100,000 inhabitants		1,950.9	197.8	1,753.2	5.9	15.6	53.8	122.4	793.3	684.4	275.4
OREGON											
Standard Metropolitan Statistical Area											
Area actually reporting	1,280,691	48,424	4,189	44,235	63	288	1,993	1,845	20,758	17,714	5,763
	100.0%										
Other cities	346,952										
Area actually reporting	99.5%	7,903	556	7,347	10	38	80	428	3,109	3,476	762
Estimated total	100.0%	7,941	558	7,383	10	38	80	430	3,124	3,493	766
Rural	463,742										
Area actually reporting	99.6%	6,087	624	5,463	24	51	71	478	2,739	2,294	430
Estimated total	100.0%	6,111	626	5,485	24	51	71	480	2,750	2,303	432
State total	2,091,385	62,476	5,373	57,103	97	377	2,144	2,755	26,632	23,510	6,961
Rate per 100,000 inhabitants		2,987.3	256.9	2,730.4	4.6	18.0	102.5	131.7	1,273.4	1,124.1	332.8

Area	Population	Crime Index total	Violent crime [1]	Property crime [2]	Murder	Forcible rape	Robbery	Aggravated assault	Burglary	Larceny $50 and over	Auto theft
PENNSYLVANIA											
Standard Metropolitan Statistical Area	9,365,552										
Area actually reporting	93.4%	150,377	22,803	127,574	567	1,141	11,833	9,262	55,171	36,200	36,203
Estimated total	100.0%	159,074	23,535	135,539	578	1,182	12,115	9,660	58,477	39,137	37,925
Other cities	923,401										
Area actually reporting	87.6%	9,094	641	8,453	16	26	179	420	3,591	3,675	1,187
Estimated total	100.0%	10,386	732	9,654	18	30	204	480	4,101	4,197	1,356
Rural	1,504,956										
Area actually reporting	100.0%	12,321	765	11,556	33	122	180	430	7,508	3,222	826
State total	11,793,909	181,781	25,032	156,749	629	1,334	12,499	10,570	70,086	46,556	40,107
Rate per 100,000 inhabitants		1,541.3	212.2	1,329.1	5.3	11.3	106.0	89.6	594.3	394.7	340.1
RHODE ISLAND											
Standard Metropolitan Statistical Area	769,789										
Area actually reporting	100.0%	23,342	1,610	21,732	28	30	644	908	8,004	6,093	7,635
Other cities	176,200										
Area actually reporting	100.0%	4,195	311	3,884	2	1	99	209	1,556	1,841	487
Rural	3,734										
Area actually reporting	100.0%	250	23	227		3	1	19	117	74	36
State total	949,723	27,787	1,944	25,843	30	34	744	1,136	9,677	8,008	8,158
Rate per 100,000 inhabitants		2,925.8	204.7	2,721.1	3.2	3.6	78.3	119.6	1,018.9	843.2	859.0
SOUTH CAROLINA											
Standard Metropolitan Statistical Area	1,017,254										
Area actually reporting	97.6%	28,948	3,713	25,235	143	228	1,125	2,217	12,390	8,713	4,132
Estimated total	100.0%	29,490	3,770	25,720	145	229	1,140	2,256	12,611	8,932	4,177
Other cities	445,589										
Area actually reporting	78.3%	8,842	1,276	7,566	44	71	173	988	3,659	3,037	870
Estimated total	100.0%	11,294	1,630	9,664	56	91	221	1,262	4,674	3,879	1,111
Rural	1,127,673										
Area actually reporting	51.6%	6,578	1,025	5,553	91	64	100	770	3,187	1,800	566
Estimated total	100.0%	12,756	1,987	10,769	176	124	194	1,493	6,181	3,491	1,097
State total	2,590,516	53,540	7,387	46,153	377	444	1,555	5,011	23,466	16,302	6,385
Rate per 100,000 inhabitants		2,066.8	285.2	1,781.6	14.6	17.1	60.0	193.4	905.8	629.3	246.5

[1] Violent crime is offenses of murder, forcible rape, robbery, and aggravated assault.

[2] Property crime is offenses of burglary, larceny $50 and over, and auto theft.

For standard metropolitan statistical areas in this table the percentage actually reporting may not coincide with the ratio between reported and estimated crime totals since these data represent the sum of such calculations for individual areas varying in size, portions reporting, and crime rates.

Population is 1970 census.

ous to the traveler, it seems, as Central Park in New York City is today. The Kentucky legislature had the foresight to realize that a man was entitled to protect himself. This is more than can be said for New York lawmakers whose position supports the Central Park muggers more strongly than the innocent citizens who fear to walk the streets alone.

The New York Sullivan Law, named for Timothy D. Sullivan, the former Democratic Tammany Hall organization leader, dates back to 1911. The law was particularly useful in its early days when it served to send criminals "up the river" in cases where no other charges could be proven. It was common knowledge in New York, too, that guns could be "planted" by police on the premises of those individuals whom the administration wanted to take out of circulation for a while.

Today, it is next to impossible for the honest citizen to obtain a permit to purchase and own a handgun in New York. He must fill out a lengthy application form, one which the authorities themselves are evidently not very proud of. A representative whose residence is in New York City attempted to obtain a copy of this application; he was refused by the officers in charge of the 61st, 69th, and 71st Police Precincts. He was also unable to obtain this form from City Hall. In each case, he was told the form would not be released unless he "qualified" for a handgun. To qualify, one must be a law-enforcement officer, a bank guard, or a person whose business re-

40

quires extraordinary sums of cash to be carried on his person. Three references must be provided and each must sign sworn statements relating their knowledge of the applicant, his character, and their own character. Multiple copies of a photograph must be included as well.

Under unusual circumstances, gun club members can obtain permits for regularly scheduled target practice meets, but the red tape is phenomenal. Waits of three to six months are typically reported by New York applicants.

Since 1911, numerous amendments to the Sullivan Law have been tacked on, piecemeal, in an effort to further reduce gun ownership. Crime rates continued to soar despite these additions. The term "weapon" has come to mean a multitude of things, including hat pins, letter openers, tear-gas canisters and rolls of coins, to name a few. Prosecutions have been conducted frequently against individuals, even after one of these "concealed weapons" was shown to have warded off a criminal attack.

Fortunately, the national scene is not plagued with the kinds of problems which permeate New York City, but gun legislation on this level has been equally ineffective in stopping crime. During the first one hundred fifty years of existence, the United States had no federal laws restricting gun ownership or possession. Indeed, the very first such law was passed in 1934. It looked more like a tax levy than a gun control measure because it imposed heavy taxes on automatic weapons, sawed-off shotguns, cut-down rifles, silencers, and gadget guns (those disguised as flashlights or other oddities). Gangland-style killings with automatic weapons continue to this day, nonetheless.

In 1938, the Federal Firearms Act became law. Manufacturers, importers, and dealers in firearms were required to register with the government, paying a modest fee. But the individual owner was not required to register the guns in his possession. It was only because of strong National Rifle Association prodding that this individual registration feature did not become part of the law. Firearms and ammunition were covered by this bill. Shipment through the mails of guns or bullets in interstate commerce to a felon, someone under indictment, a fugitive from justice, or someone not having a local permit was prohibited. Dealers were required to maintain permanent records of all transactions.

The law did not stop minors from purchasing guns, nor for that matter, alcoholics, drug addicts, or the insane. Indeed, the law did not even stop felons and fugitives from receiving guns because the dealer was only prohibited from selling to "known" felons or fugitives. This could never be proven after a sale.

In 1954, the Mutual Security Act gave the President the power to limit imports or exports of firearms or ammunition. While this prevented large-scale movements of weapons across our borders, customs regulations still allowed Americans the right to bring in three firearms and one thousand rounds of ammunition.

On April 28, 1958, John F. Kennedy, then a Senator from Massachusetts, introduced a bill in Congress which would have prohibited the "importation of firearms originally manufactured for military purposes." The proposed law would have protected the Democratic Senator's home state where firearms manufacture is a significantly important industry. The law failed to pass, but a substitute measure prohibiting the import of weapons which the United States had originally shipped overseas as part of its aid program became law.

In 1963, Senator Thomas J. Dodd introduced a bill in Congress which would have required a mail-order purchaser of handguns to furnish the seller a statement that he was over eighteen years of age, not a convicted felon nor under indictment for a felony, and that the shipment of the firearm would in no way violate any local law or ordinance. Upon the assassination of President Kennedy, the Dodd Bill was amended to include shotguns and rifles. Additionally, a registration procedure would have required that the seller notify the "chief law enforcement officer" in the buyer's community of the sale. In effect, the police would have tabs on the purchase and ownership of all guns.

In a 1968 *New Yorker* article by Richard Harris, the author stated that the Commerce Committee received in a two-week period twenty thousand letters, postcards and telegrams in opposition to this bill. Two communications were received in support. Senator Dodd evidently had as much trouble convincing the American people of the need or desirability of this legislation as he later had convincing his own Democratic Party members and others in the Congress that he had not engaged in gross impropriety while in office.

In 1965, Senator Dodd introduced a proposal by the Johnson Administration which would have prohibited completely the interstate mail-order sale of firearms to individuals, prohibited the over-the-counter sale of handguns to out-of-state persons, stopped importation of firearms deemed unsuitable for "sporting" purposes, and prevented people under twenty-one years of age from purchasing handguns (eighteen for rifles and shotguns). This kind of bill would have clearly done the most damage in rural areas of the nation where mail-order or out-of-state travel to purchase a gun is commonplace.

An identical bill was introduced in the House of Representatives, but no bill was reported out of committee nor acted upon. The public was clearly against losing its right to keep and bear arms. But the politicians did not stop there.

In August of 1966, psychotic Charles Whitman fired upon a crowd of people from the University of Texas Tower, killing or injuring over forty bystanders. The President quickly grabbed hold of the issue, trying to take advantage of the emotional involve-

44

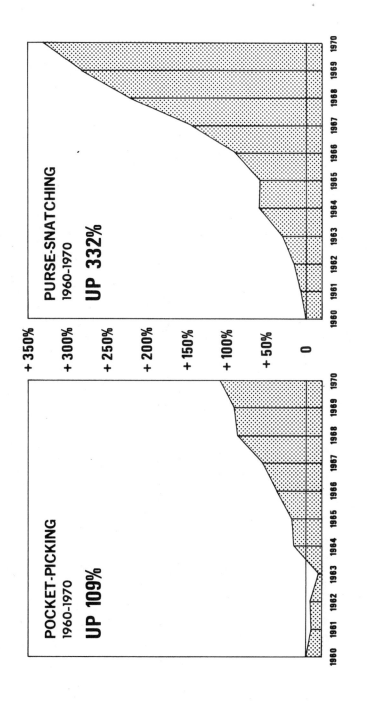

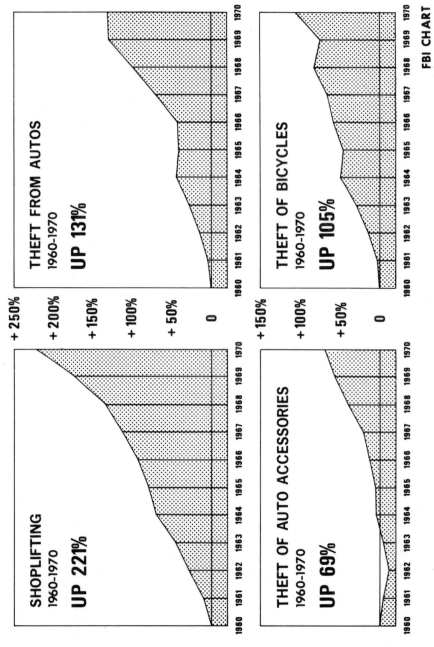

SHOPLIFTING
1960-1970
UP 221%

THEFT FROM AUTOS
1960-1970
UP 131%

THEFT OF AUTO ACCESSORIES
1960-1970
UP 69%

THEFT OF BICYCLES
1960-1970
UP 105%

FBI CHART

46

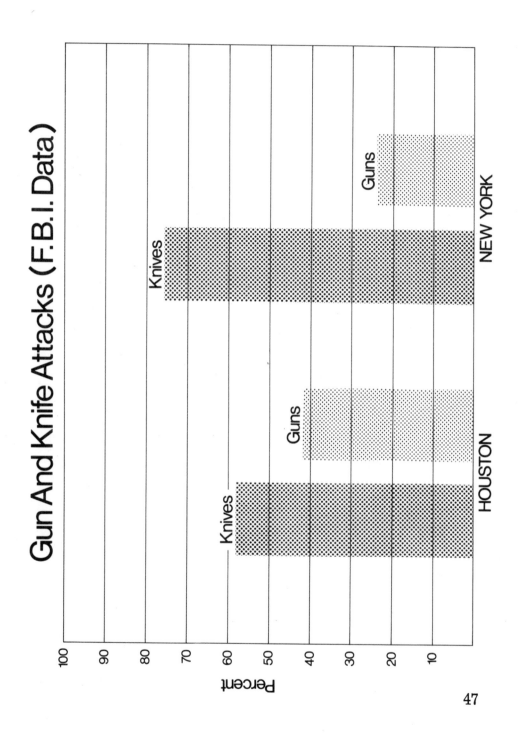

Gun And Knife Attacks (F.B.I. Data)

47

ment Americans had as a result of the news coverage this story received. This was the same tactic employed when President Kennedy was felled by an assassin's bullet. Americans were too sharp to believe that any amount of legislation could have impeded the wishes of either Oswald or Whitman, however.

President Johnson, again after a tragic death—this time, the killing of Senator Robert F. Kennedy on June 5, 1968, called on Congress to impose harsh laws on gun ownership or sales and also asked that the individual states enact their own stringent laws. As a result of this appeal, he signed the *Omnibus Crime Control and Safe Streets Act of 1968* which contained new restrictions on firearms. Ironically enough, the incidence of street crime continued to rise sharply, according to recent FBI statistics.

The 1968 Act, among other things, made it illegal for felons, dishonorably discharged veterans, mental incompetents, aliens illegally in this country, and former citizens who have renounced their citizenship to receive or possess firearms. Penalties were set at a maximum of two years imprisonment and a $10,000 fine.

The President was still clamoring for a stronger bill which would lead the way toward the eventual disarming of American citizens, but Congress was not receptive. It was 1968, an election year. While the legislative body refused to go along with Mr. Johnson's proposed federal registration of all firearms, including shotguns and rifles, it did enact the Gun Control Act of 1968. This second measure revised the Omnibus Crime Bill.

Among its provisions were higher standards for obtaining firearms licenses and increased fees; prohibition on the receipt or transportation in interstate commerce of a firearm by felons, fugitives from justice, unlawful users of certain drugs, persons adjudicated to be mental defectives, or persons previously committed to a mental institution; and shipment with intent to commit an unlawful criminal act. The use of a gun so received for an unlawful act was now met with severe penalties ranging from one year to life, depending on whether the offense was a first or second offense. A second offender could not be given a suspended or probationary sentence. The Act did not apply to guns loaned or sold through the National Board for the Promotion of Rifle Practice. The new law also provided for the ownership of firearm "curios and relics" and "war souvenirs" by members of the armed forces.

The current impetus in gun control legislation, nonetheless, is still aimed at disarming the honest, law-abiding citizen. *We know that guns are used in only 3 percent of the total number of crimes committed.* The American Bar Foundation, an offshoot of the American Bar Association, published a report which said that there was no link between gun availability and increased crime. After studying the New

York State Sullivan Law, one would independently arrive at this conclusion.

No amount of legislation aimed at the registration or confiscation of guns of the honest American citizen would have saved the lives of President Kennedy, his brother Robert, or Dr. Martin Luther King. No law shoved down the throats of American citizens would have prevented the shooting of Alabama Governor George Wallace.

Indeed, it was Wallace himself, in April 1972, who told a group of sportsmen in Detroit that legislators in the individual states and Congressmen in Washington respond most "to groups who make the most noise. . . ." He said that "disarming of the American citizen in violation of the Constitution" is something to which just a few loud militants address themselves, in opposition to the wishes of most law-abiding Americans.

Assassins or potential assassins in the United States, like in Africa and South America where political upheaval often finds its roots in violence, will not be deterred by gun laws. *There is no practical means by which all guns currently in the hands of Americans can be accounted for or confiscated, regardless of the penalties imposed for unlawful possession.* Such laws are the pipedreams of politicians who refuse to accept the realities of life—criminals will not be disarmed by signed bills in Washington.

One such proposed measure was introduced by Democratic Senator Philip Hart of Michigan. Introducing it early in November 1971, the Senator admitted in the *Congressional Record* that only 99 letters reaching his office expressed favorable interest in the kind of bill he was introducing, compared with the 607 letters disapproving of the measure. But like many others on Capitol Hill, Mr. Hart did not feel he had to be particularly responsive to the wishes of his constituents, once elected.

Manipulating statistics, the Senator stated that "only 2 percent of home robberies and 1 percent of home burglaries result in the intruder being shot by the householder." This he termed "minimal protection." To those families who protected their lives and properties through gun ownership when confronted by the criminal robber or burglar, the protection was hardly "minimal." If many more American homeowners were encouraged, rather than discouraged, from owning protective firearms, the incidence of robbery, burglary, and other violent crimes might be reduced dramatically. It has often been said that the *astronomical crime rates in New York City derive directly from the criminal's knowledge that the homeowner is apt to be unprotected.*

In any case, Senator Hart's proposal was aimed at disarming all Americans once and for all. The law-abiding citizen would be given just six months in which to turn in his handguns to the Federal government. After that period of time, a citizen still possessing one of these weapons might find himself behind bars for five years, shy five thousand dollars, or both. The penalties, it seems, are generally harsher than those imposed on criminals who misuse guns in the commission of crimes.

The bill's sponsor admitted that it would "doubtless take many years" for such a law to achieve its desired effect. More likely, the only effect of this bill would be the shifting of statistical gun ownership *from the homes of law-abiding citizens to the arsenals of organized crime.*

The attempts at gun control legislation go on and on. It is up to each citizen to be aware of impending legislation. He should make his feelings known to his lawmakers both on the state and federal level and check his legislator's voting record.

Since the Gun Control Act of 1968 passed Congress during the emotional aftermath of the murder of Robert F. Kennedy, conscientious lawmakers have tried repeatedly to soften one of the harshest portions of the bill.

When the important ammunition recordkeeping amendment came before the House of Representatives on December 21, 1970, obviously 128 Members had more pressing matters at that time of year. They were not present to vote.

This amendment to the Gun Control Act was to exempt recordkeeping by licensed gun dealers of all ammunition sales for "shotgun ammunition, ammunition suitable for use only in rifles, .22 caliber rimfire ammunition, or component parts for the aforesaid types of ammunition." Backing the plea of the

91ST CONGRESS
1ST SESSION

H. R. 14233

IN THE HOUSE OF REPRESENTATIVES

OCTOBER 7, 1969

MR. ULLMAN introduced the following bill; which was referred to the Committee on Ways and Means

A BILL

To modify ammunition recordkeeping requirements.

1 *Be it enacted by the Senate and House of Representa-*
2 *tives of the United States of America in Congress assembled,*
3 That section 4182 of title 26 of the United States Code is
4 amended by adding the following subsection (c):
5 "(c) RECORDS.—Notwithstanding the provisions of sec-
6 tions 922 (b) (5) and 923 (g) of title 18, United States
7 Code, no person holding a Federal license under chapter 44
8 of title 18, United States Code, shall be required to record
9 the name, address, or other information about the purchaser
10 of shotgun ammunition, ammunition suitable for use only in
11 rifles, .22 caliber rimfire ammunition, or component parts
12 for the aforesaid types of ammunition."

bill's sponsor, Representative Al Ullman, against the monumental paperwork involved in such record-keeping was a statement from the Department of Justice:

> There is not a single known instance, as we have learned from our discussions with the Internal Revenue Service, with the firearms people there, not a single known instance where any of the record keeping has led to a successful investigation and prosecution of a crime.

As of this writing, the exemption has not yet been passed by Congress, due to indifference similar to that of these Representatives who could not be bothered to attend a vote just before Christmas.

The reader cannot for one moment believe that attempted gun control is a thing of the past. Its proponents are active today, trying to disarm the public. Shortly after the shooting of Governor Wallace occurred, pressure was brought to bear on our President to propose measures which would outlaw the so-called "Saturday night special" guns. This refers to cheap guns, many imported, and some said to be lacking in safety standards. Such a bill would not hurt the legitimate sportsman or homeowner since an unsafe gun can be more harmful than helpful to the law-abiding citizen. But the fact is that such a law in effect would not have prevented the shooting of Governor Wallace, nor for that matter, of President Kennedy.

The SPEAKER. The question is on the motion of the gentleman from Oregon (Mr. ULLMAN) that the House suspend the rules and pass the bill, H.R. 14233, as amended.

The question was taken.

Mr. BINGHAM. Mr. Speaker, I object to the vote on the ground that a quorum is not present and make the point of order that a quorum is not present.

The SPEAKER. Evidently a quorum is not present.

The Doorkeeper will close the doors, the Sergeant at Arms will notify absent Members and the Clerk will call the roll.

The question was taken; and there were—yeas 246, nays 59, not voting 128, as follows:

[Roll No. 435]

YEAS—246

Abernethy
Albert
Alexander
Anderson, Calif.
Anderson, Ill.
Anderson, Tenn.
Andrews, Ala.
Annunzio
Arends
Baring
Beall, Md.
Bennett
Betts
Bevill
Blackburn
Blanton
Blatnik
Boggs
Boland
Bow
Bray
Brinkley
Broomfield
Brotzman
Brown, Mich.
Brown, Ohio
Broyhill, N.C.

Fuqua
Garmatz
Gaydos
Gettys
Giaimo
Goldwater
Gonzalez
Goodling
Gray
Green, Oreg.
Griffin
Gross
Grover
Gubser

Broyhill, Va.
Buchanan
Burleson, Tex.
Bush
Byrnes, Wis.
Carney
Carter
Casey
Cederberg
Chamberlain
Chappell
Clark
Cleveland
Collier
Collins, Tex.
Colmer
Conable
Conte
Culver
Cunningham
Daniel, Va.
Davis, Ga.
Davis, Wis.
dè la Garza
Dellenback
Dennis
Derwinski
Dickinson
Dingell

McCloskey
McClure
McDade
McDonald, Mich.
McEwen
McFall
Macdonald, Mass.
MacGregor
Madden
Mahon
Mailliard
Mann

Dorn
Downing
Dulski
Duncan
Eckhardt
Edmondson
Edwards, Ala.
Edwards, La.
Erlenborn
Esch
Eshleman
Evans, Colo.
Feighan
Findley
Fisher
Flood
Flowers
Flynt
Foley
Ford, Gerald R.
Ford, William D.
Foreman
Forsythe
Fountain
Frelinghuysen
Frey
Friedel
Fulton, Pa.

Rooney, Pa.
Roth
Sandman
Schadeberg
Schmitz
Schneebeli
Schwengel
Scott
Sebelius
Shriver
Sisk
Skubitz
Slack
Smith, Calif.

Hagan
Hamilton
Hammer- schmidt
Hanley
Hanna
Hansen, Idaho
Harsha
Harvey
Hays
Heckler, Mass.
Henderson
Hicks
Hogan
Hosmer
Hunt
Hutchinson
Ichord
Jacobs
Jarman
Johnson, Calif.
Johnson, Pa.
Jonas
Jones, Ala.
Jones, N.C.
Jones, Tenn.
Karth
Kazen
Kee
Keith
King
Kleppe
Kluczynski
Kuykendall
Kyl
Kyros
Landgrebe
Leggett
Lennon
Lloyd
Long, Md.

Marsh
Mayne
Meeds
Melcher
Miller, Ohio
Minshall
Mizell
Mollohan
Moorhead
Morgan
Myers
Natcher
Nedzi
Nelsen
Nichols
Obey
O'Hara
Olsen
Passman
Patten
Pepper
Perkins
Pickle
Pirnie
Poage
Poff
Preyer, N.C.
Price, Ill.
Pryor, Ark.
Pucinski
Purcell
Quie
Quillen
Railsback
Randall
Reid, Ill.
Riegle
Roberts
Robison
Rogers, Colo.
Rogers, Fla.

Smith, Iowa
Smith, N.Y.
Springer
Stafford
Staggers
Stanton
Steed
Steiger, Wis.
Stratton
Stubblefield
Stuckey
Talcott
Taylor
Teague, Calif.
Teague, Tex.
Thompson, Ga.
Thomson, Wis.
Udall
Ullman
Van Deerlin
Vander Jagt
Vigorito
Wampler
Ware
Watson
Watts
Whalen
Whalley
White
Whitehurst
Whitten
Widnall
Wiggins
Williams
Wright
Wyatt
Wylie
Wyman
Yatron
Zablocki
Zion

NAYS—59

Adams
Addabbo
Ashley
Bell, Calif.
Biaggi
Biester
Bingham
Bolling
Brademas
Brasco
Burke, Mass.
Burton, Calif.
Byrne, Pa.
Carey
Celler
Cohelan
Conyers
Corman
Daniels, N.J.
Donohue

Eilberg
Fraser
Gallagher
Green, Pa.
Gude
Harrington
Hathaway
Hechler, W. Va.
Helstoski
Holifield
Howard
Kastenmeier
Koch
Lowenstein
Matsunaga
Mikva
Minish
Mink
Morse
Mosher

Murphy, N.Y.
Nix
O'Neill, Mass.
Philbin
Pike
Podell
Rees
Reid, N.Y.
Rodino
Rooney, N.Y.
Rosenthal
Roybal
Ryan
Scheuer
Symington
Thompson, N.J.
Tiernan
Vanik
Yates

THE CRIME SCENE

Statistics show that more violent crime is committed in the United States than in any other nation the world over. Using figures from 1970 Uniform Crime Reports compiled by the FBI, our homicide rate stands at 7.8 per 100,000 population, up 8.4% since 1969. This means that nearly 16,000 persons were murdered in 1970.

Supporters of gun control legislation have attempted to link these high crime rates with the availability of guns in this country. Their attempts are without merit for several reasons. If we turn, for example, to Switzerland, we shall find that a substantially lower crime rate exists despite the larger number of available guns in civilian hands.

Indeed, Switzerland is a country of universal military training, often referred to as "the country of the rifleman." Every able-bodied male of age is issued a rifle, since the country maintains no regular standing armies. Interestingly enough, Switzerland also has managed not only to maintain a homicide

National Crime, Rate, and Percent Change

Crime Index offenses	Estimated crime 1970		Percent change over 1969		Percent change over 1965		Percent change over 1960	
	Number	Rate per 100,000 inhabitants	Number	Rate	Number	Rate	Number	Rate
Total	5,568,200	2,740.5	+11.3	+10.6	+90.0	+81.3	+176.4	+143.9
Violent	731,400	360.0	+11.7	+11.0	+90.9	+82.2	+156.5	+126.4
Property	4,836,800	2,380.5	+11.3	+10.6	+89.9	+81.1	+179.7	+146.8
Murder	15,810	7.8	+8.4	+8.3	+60.5	+52.9	+75.7	+56.0
Forcible rape	37,270	18.3	+2.2	+1.1	+62.3	+53.8	+121.1	+94.7
Robbery	348,380	171.5	+17.1	+16.4	+152.3	+140.5	+224.4	+186.3
Aggravated assault	329,940	162.4	+7.7	+7.0	+55.6	+48.3	+117.1	+91.7
Burglary	2,169,300	1,067.7	+11.3	+10.6	+71.9	+64.0	+141.7	+113.3
Larceny $50 and over	1,746,100	859.4	+14.5	+13.8	+120.4	+110.2	+244.9	+204.4
Auto theft	921,400	453.5	+5.7	+5.0	+86.9	+78.3	+182.9	+149.7

rate less than half that of the United States, but it has maintained its independence and neutrality. An armed people is a definite deterrent to military take-over from outside one's borders.

There are well over thirty million gun owners in the United States, most of them living outside of the largest cities. Many are collectors of firearms, who take pride in showing the guns which played so great a role in America's earlier days. Most of these owners are also avid hunters who enjoy the exercise and challenge of the sport for fun and food.

Yet statistics show that most violent crime is centered in the largest cities where guns are not heavily concentrated. About 17 percent of our entire population—in about two dozen major cities—contribute to nearly half the total reported major crimes of violence. There must be a link to crime other than firearms, and there is.

Large cities are plagued by overcrowding, poor living conditions, substandard education, and tensions between people. Racial problems usually originate in the city. Riots take place in the city. A greater percentage of emotional disorders are reported in the cities.

Guns are no more the core of violent crime than is the position of the sun in the sky. The illegal use of drugs, parents who refuse to accept responsibility for their children, overcrowded jails, and courts which mete out very light sentences putting crim-

Murder by circumstance

[Percent distribution]

Region	Total	Spouse killing spouse	Parent killing child	Other family killings	Romantic triangle and lovers quarrels	Other arguments	Known felony type	Suspected felony type
Northeastern States	100.0	9.6	3.7	6.1	7.9	38.4	25.4	8.9
North Central States	100.0	11.3	3.0	8.9	5.0	39.5	22.4	9.9
Southern States	100.0	13.8	2.2	8.8	8.4	46.0	13.9	6.9
Western States	100.0	12.5	4.9	7.0	6.4	32.2	28.0	9.0
Total	100.0	12.1	3.1	8.1	7.1	40.8	20.4	8.4

inals back on the streets, are more responsible for crime than firearms.

The gun has been used as a scapegoat by the inept politician who hopes to rally support around an emotional cause. When a public figure says that gun control is the answer to our crime problems, he is merely saying he is unable to tackle the *real* problem at the root of crime.

It has also been shown that violent crimes of homicide, assault and rape occur most frequently among relatives, close friends and acquaintances. These are often crimes of passion—broken love affairs, jealousies and hatreds. If the attacker does not have a gun at his disposal, then a knife, a razor, a rope, a chain, or poison can take its toll. The knife alone has been used in nearly one fourth of all homicides, according to official statistics.

Even when persons band together to commit crimes, many means other than firearms are available to them to inflict damage, serious injury, or death. The Democratic National Convention in Chicago during August of 1968 is a good example. What started out as a traditional American institution of democratic government—a party's nomination for the Presidency—ended in total disaster. Demonstrators disrupted the convention and the city with police confrontations arising at streetcorner after streetcorner.

Despite the publicity that the affair received, little was said about the extent of police injuries and

A CHOICE OF WEAPONS—Many tools of violent crime and murder are used against the law-abiding citizen. Guns play only a very small part in all attacks and violent crimes.

the kinds of weapons used to inflict them. A dozen officers of the law reported burns from chemicals hurled at them, four were bitten by demonstrators, one was stabbed, eyes were gouged, faces scratched with fingernails, and hundreds hit by flying objects tossed by demonstrators. These missiles hurled by demonstrators included rocks, bricks, cans, bottles, knives, shoes with embedded razors, bags of urine, and other sordid materials. Hundreds of police and demonstrator injuries were reported during the one-week period, *but not a single gun was reported to have been used in an illegal fashion during the melee.*

Of over 600 persons arrested, 118 had previous arrest records. *Guns did no damage. People did.* A certain breed of individual was responsible for the devastation. Had some of these demonstrators been amply punished when they had their previous problems with the law, they might not have come to Chicago with violence in mind.

In New York City, the strict Sullivan Law virtually denies the right of the individual to own a gun. As a result, fewer than 20,000 (approximately ¼ of 1 percent) of the city's eight million residents are entitled to possess handguns. In many states, the right to carry a concealed handgun is curtailed, but in New York, the right to own one—even for protection in one's home has been denied. FBI statistics show clearly that New York City has one of the highest records of violent crimes. But more importantly, innocent New Yorkers are subject to the greatest risks in walking the streets or maintaining businesses because they cannot defend themselves. The police themselves have repeatedly refused to "walk the beat" alone in many areas. They travel in large groups when in Central Park, once a showplace of serenity for Manhattan-dwellers, now a haven for muggers.

Taxicab holdups in New York reached horrendous proportions, and many a "cabbie" was mourned by his fellow workers after a senseless execution-robbery combination. *The police department followed through with a directive allowing New York City policemen to drive taxis, out of uniform, when off duty. To nobody's surprise, assaults and robberies on taxi drivers dropped when the criminals realized the consequences of a driver up front who might be armed.*

In Philadelphia, Mayor Frank Rizzo, like New York's Mayor John Lindsay, saw guns as a potential threat to the community. Philadelphia was the scene of many gang-related murders and disturbances. The Mayor, once police commissioner of that city, felt he had the answer. An amnesty was declared in the early months of 1972, during which gang members were encouraged to turn in weapons, without prosecution for their illegal possession. It was announced that after the amnesty period, severe crackdowns would begin and prosecutions would follow.

The amnesty had to be extended because of the total failure of the initial collection phase. Only after members of the community pleaded on radio and television for gang members to comply with the Democratic mayor, did weapons start to come in. They did not pour in. Nobody beat a path to the Mayor's door. *In fact, only a handful of arms were ever turned over to the police in what amounted to an apparent failure.* It is doubtful that one gun in a thousand was removed from the gangs by the amnesty, despite the threats of harder crackdowns in the future.

Most gun control campaigns for supposed crime reduction or prevention are aimed at handguns, primarily because they are more easily concealed. The criminal, it is believed, will have greater difficulty in engaging in a holdup with a rifle. On the other hand, who speaks for the honest shopkeeper who is interested in protecting himself and his place of business? In limiting the criminal by taking away his handguns, even if that were possible, the shopkeeper will also find protection that much more difficult.

Many merchants, like taxi drivers, are no longer alive to describe their assailants. They were disarmed by the law—in fact, by the more than 20,000 gun laws and codes in this nation—in the use of guns for protection. The shotgun or rifle is really of limited use in protecting a store or business. The quick access of a handgun is what is needed to deter this type of crime. Time after time, we learn of senseless killings for pennies, many of these occurring after the businessman has handed over his receipts.

Unfortunately, some of us do not even learn from the positive experiences citizens have had in protecting themselves, cases where these men and women *are* alive today because of gun ownership.

One young lady in New York recently warded off an individual who threatened to assault her. She used nothing more than a tear gas gun, commercially available and sold through mail order. *Despite the fact that she prevented the assault and perhaps saved her life, she was threatened with prosecution for carrying a weapon banned by the Sullivan Law.* Others who have protected themselves with knives and, in one case, a hat pin, faced similar problems.

Lawmakers often lead sheltered lives, arrange escorts for their wives, and are afforded special protection against criminal activity. It is no wonder they do not appreciate the needs of the individual citizen —the farmer, the worker, the homeowner.

We should stop and ask ourselves whether our laws are geared to protect the criminal or the law-abiding citizen. Gun control legislation will inevitably hurt the honest man most.

● In St. Louis, a couple was awakened one night to learn that an intruder was at the front door. When the elderly lady opened the door, the assailant pushed her around. Her husband came to the rescue with a .25-caliber automatic, killing the intruder with one shot.

● The *New York Daily News* recently reported the case of Charles DiMaggio, a small grocery store owner. In ten years of business, twenty-six attempted robberies were made on his place of business. Because he kept a gun behind the counter, fifteen hoodlums were captured as a result of his efforts, and three were killed.

• A nineteen-year-old in Florida attempted to break into a home occupied by a teen-age babysitter and her younger brother. Arming himself with a .22-caliber pistol, the girl's brother blew several warning shots into the floor, scaring off the intruder. When the police arrested the man who attempted to gain entrance to the house, they found that he had three prior arrests in the year preceding this incident.

• A tavern owner in Cary, Illinois, woke up to find two men burglarizing his business. He promptly reached for his handgun, took aim, and wounded one of the thugs. The police found several hundred dollars on the bleeding man.

What are the costs of crime? Human lives cannot be measured in dollars and cents. Every innocent citizen who dies because he was disarmed by an unconstitutional law, is a reprimand to each citizen.

The President's Commission on Law Enforcement and Administration of Justice reported in one recent year that crimes against the person—homicides and assaults—cost $815,000,000. This is the dollar amount of lost wages and earnings as a result of these crimes, and in no way can measure the accompanying grief and despair.

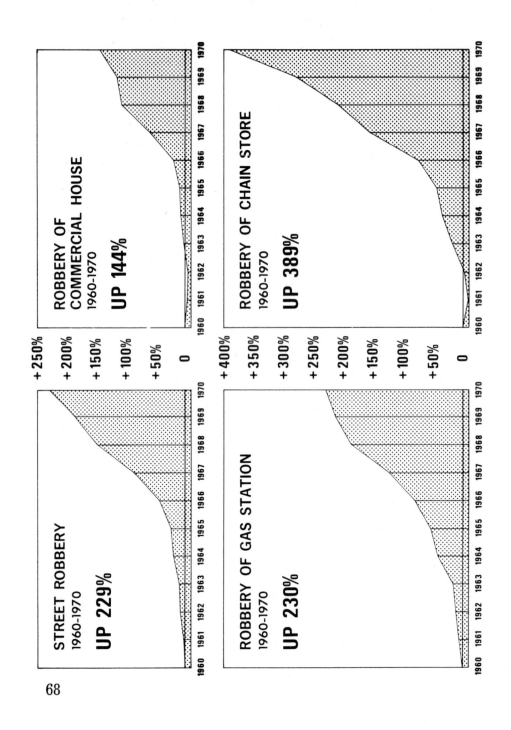

STREET ROBBERY
1960-1970
UP 229%

ROBBERY OF COMMERCIAL HOUSE
1960-1970
UP 144%

ROBBERY OF GAS STATION
1960-1970
UP 230%

ROBBERY OF CHAIN STORE
1960-1970
UP 389%

68

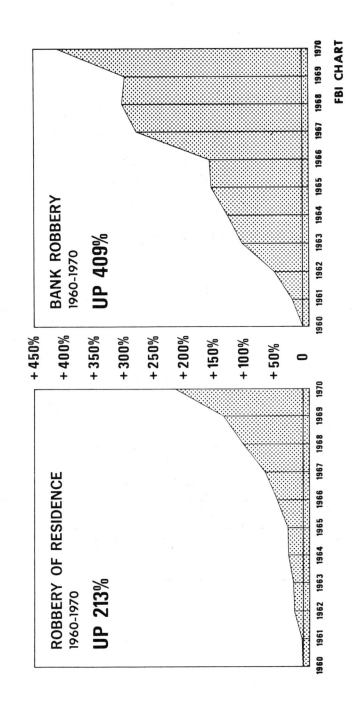

ROBBERY OF RESIDENCE
1960-1970

UP 213%

BANK ROBBERY
1960-1970

UP 409%

FBI CHART

69

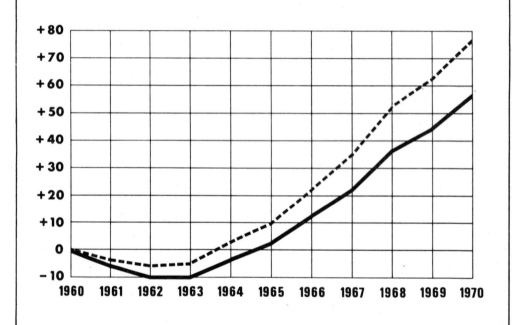

MURDER
1960 - 1970

PERCENT CHANGE OVER 1960

- - - - - NUMBER OF OFFENSES UP 76 PERCENT
———— RATE PER 100,000 INHABITANTS UP 56 PERCENT

FBI CHART

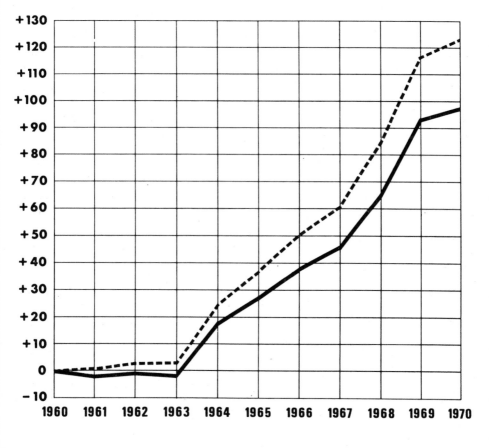

FORCIBLE RAPE
1960 - 1970

PERCENT CHANGE OVER 1960
- - - - - NUMBER OF OFFENSES UP 121 PERCENT
———— RATE PER 100,000 INHABITANTS UP 95 PERCENT

FBI CHART

71

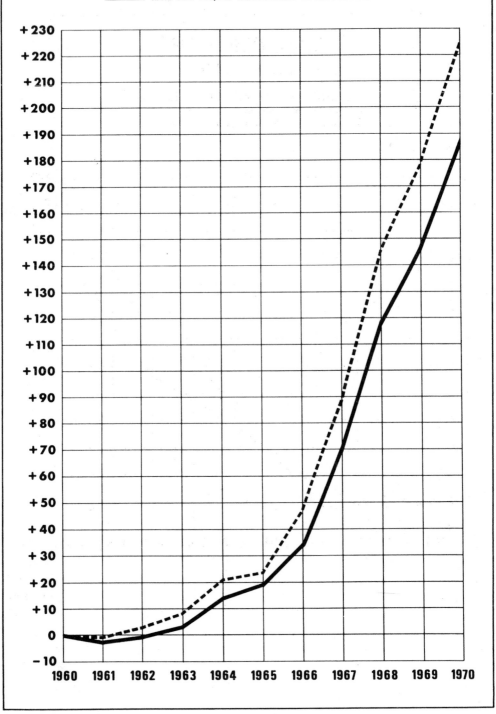

ROBBERY
1960 - 1970

PERCENT CHANGE OVER 1960
- - - - - NUMBER OF OFFENSES UP 224 PERCENT
———— RATE PER 100,000 INHABITANTS UP 186 PERCENT

Crimes against property were still more expensive—$3,932,000,000. If you were one of the businessmen or homeowners who lost part of these hard-earned dollars, you would undoubtedly wish you could have done something about it. If you were the victim of a successful holdup or robbery, gun protection could have changed the outcome.

The Federal Bureau of Investigation reported that serious crimes increased dramatically over the period 1960 to 1970. Murders increased 76 percent, manslaughter over 80 percent, rape better than 120 percent, and robbery figures almost 224 percent! These figures far exceed population growths. They surely do not represent greater ease in obtaining weapons. On the contrary, gun control legislation made gun ownership more difficult during this period.

Ten thousand people are arrested every year in this country on charges of murder or nonnegligent manslaughter. While nobody can say with certainty how many of these violent crimes would not have taken place had the law-abiding citizen been better armed, we do know that fewer innocent people would have landed in the morgue had they been better protected.

Critics of guns also state with frequency the dangers they see in accidental injuries and deaths. The United States Department of Health, Education, and Welfare statistics show death rates (per 100,000 resident population) for a number of accident types.

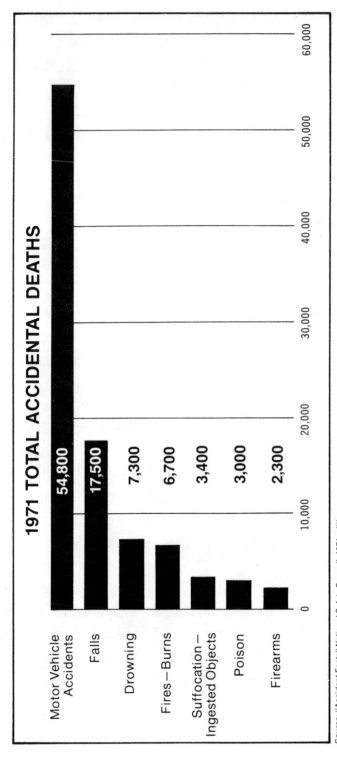

1971 TOTAL ACCIDENTAL DEATHS

Motor Vehicle Accidents	54,800
Falls	17,500
Drowning	7,300
Fires — Burns	6,700
Suffocation — Ingested Objects	3,400
Poison	3,000
Firearms	2,300

Source: "Accident Facts" National Safety Council, 1971 edition.

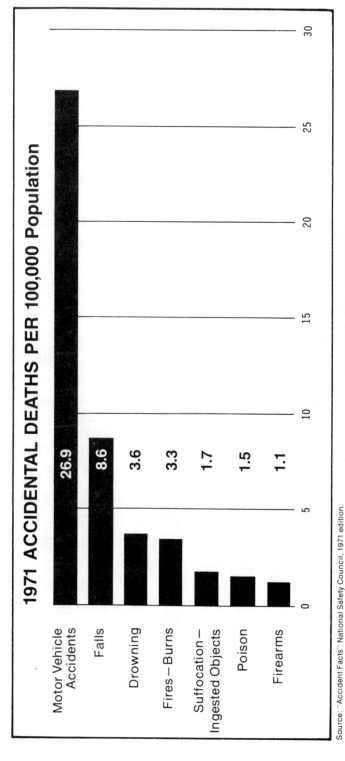

1971 ACCIDENTAL DEATHS PER 100,000 Population

Motor Vehicle Accidents	26.9
Falls	8.6
Drowning	3.6
Fires—Burns	3.3
Suffocation—Ingested Objects	1.7
Poison	1.5
Firearms	1.1

Source: "Accident Facts" National Safety Council, 1971 edition.

FIREARMS AND ACCIDENTS
Firearms accidents are but a small fraction of all accidental deaths in our county. The 2,300 known firearm deaths in 1971 ranked only seventh among all accidental deaths in the United States.

In 1968, for example, some rates were 27.5 for motor vehicle accidents, 9.3 for accidental falls, 3.0 for accidental drownings, 4.0 for fire and explosion, and only 1.2 for firearms-related deaths. Additionally, firearms play a smaller role today in accidental killings than ever, with the rate dropping from 1.4 in 1950 to 1.3 in 1955, and finally leveling off at a rate of 1.2 after 1968. *People who own guns have respect for them.*

By contrast, a seemingly unimportant source of accidental death, inhalation and ingestion of objects, increased dramatically in rate of 0.9 to 1.6 during this same period. The presence of a gun in the home, then, under proper care and supervision, is far less likely than the chance of an accidental fall from a stepladder, an automobile accident returning from a shopping trip, or an explosion caused by a faulty home heating system.

The key to gun safety is in safe practices, the kind taught by numerous organizations, including the National Rifle Association. Like any other tool, a gun carries certain responsibilities. One would not expect it to be left around for youngsters to play with, but by the same token, one would not allow a six-year-old to take the family car out for a drive.

WHO LOSES WITH GUN CONTROL?

The FBI's frightening crime clocks indicate that violent crime can and does occur any time of the night or day. Further statistics show that while certain areas have more crime than others, no portion of the country is immune from violence.

Rural dwellers have long been accustomed to reading newspaper accounts of big-city mayhem. June 15, 1972, brought two disgruntled former employees back to a swank suburban restaurant just at closing. Tieing up the employees still in the building, they proceeded to stab the owner and the assistant manager to death before the horrified eyes of the staff.

The town? Chicago. Over the years, the scene of thousands of homicides, many of them spectacularly violent. If a double knifing can ever be typical, this tragedy was just the sort that typifies the crime-ridden urban areas for most rural Americans. The

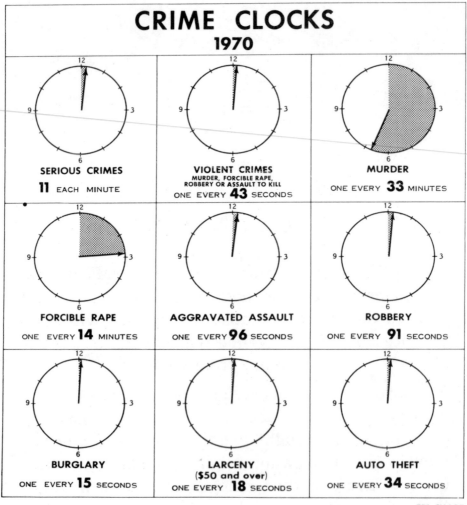

CRIME CLOCKS
1970

SERIOUS CRIMES	VIOLENT CRIMES MURDER, FORCIBLE RAPE, ROBBERY OR ASSAULT TO KILL	MURDER
11 EACH MINUTE	ONE EVERY **43** SECONDS	ONE EVERY **33** MINUTES
FORCIBLE RAPE	AGGRAVATED ASSAULT	ROBBERY
ONE EVERY **14** MINUTES	ONE EVERY **96** SECONDS	ONE EVERY **91** SECONDS
BURGLARY	LARCENY ($50 and over)	AUTO THEFT
ONE EVERY **15** SECONDS	ONE EVERY **18** SECONDS	ONE EVERY **34** SECONDS

FBI CHART

names change, the location may be in a midtown high-rise one day and in a ghetto poolroom brawl the next, but the image is the same for the farmer. Crime and big cities go hand in hand.

But in August 1971, in rural western Illinois, more than 200 miles south of the everyday violence of the nation's second largest city, a farm family was

Crime Rate by Region, 1970

[Rate per 100,000 inhabitants]

Crime Index offenses	North-eastern States	North Central States	Southern States	Western States
Total_ _ _ _ _ _ _ _	2, 845. 9	2, 398. 7	2, 400. 2	3, 761. 4
Violent _ _ _ _ _ _ _	385. 3	323. 2	362. 2	380. 0
Property_ _ _ _ _ _ _	2, 460. 6	2, 075. 5	2, 038. 0	3, 381. 3
Murder_ _ _ _ _ _ _ _	5. 8	6. 5	11. 2	6. 4
Forcible rape_ _ _ _ _	12. 7	17. 0	18. 0	28. 9
Robbery_ _ _ _ _ _ _	232. 8	172. 7	130. 2	157. 5
Aggravated assault_ _ _ _	134. 0	127. 0	202. 7	187. 3
Burglary_ _ _ _ _ _ _	1, 065. 5	896. 6	960. 7	1, 541. 8
Larceny $50 and over_ _ _	823. 2	759. 7	750. 2	1, 269. 3
Auto theft_ _ _ _ _ _	571. 9	419. 3	327. 1	570. 2

enjoying a cooling evening breeze on their front porch. A stranger approached with a gun, called out the members of the family still in the house, marched them all to the basement, and began tieing them up. The grandfather, in his seventies, protested. The still-unidentified intruder shot him and left him to bleed to death while his bound family looked on helplessly.

Thus the countryside, long considered safe from violence, is no longer an island of tranquility. Increased mobility brings the problems of the city to the doorstep of the farmyard. True isolation because of distance no longer exists in contemporary America. Since 1960, the Index of Crime for the nation in number of offenses has risen 176.4 percent from

Crime Rate by Area, 1970

[Rate per 100,000 inhabitants]

Crime Index offenses	Area			
	Total U.S.	Cities over 250,000	Suburban	Rural
Total	2,740.5	5,335.1	2,137.0	927.4
Violent	360.0	980.4	176.7	120.0
Property	2,380.5	4,354.7	1,960.3	807.4
Murder	7.8	17.5	3.8	6.4
Forcible rape	18.3	39.7	13.0	9.9
Robbery	171.5	589.4	58.3	14.1
Aggravated assault	162.4	333.9	101.6	89.6
Burglary	1,067.7	1,947.9	871.7	434.1
Larceny $50 and over	859.4	1,290.1	800.8	302.7
Auto theft	453.5	1,116.7	287.8	70.7

2,014,600 offenses to 5,568,200 offenses. All crimes except murder and nonnegligent manslaughter have more than doubled in the same ten-year period. Larceny of $50 or more has soared to a breathtaking 245 percent.

The figures available for 1971 again show large increases in the number of offenses committed over the 1970 figures. The crime rate for rural areas has again leaped 10 percent higher than for the number of offenses listed in rural areas for 1970. Rural robberies made a 19 percent rise over the preceding year's figures, the largest percentage jump for any offense regardless of the population area.

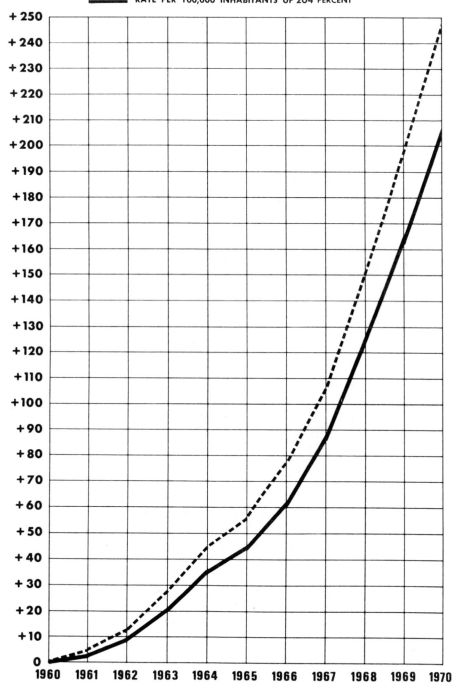

LARCENY
($50 AND OVER)
1960 - 1970

PERCENT CHANGE OVER 1960

- - - - NUMBER OF OFFENSES UP 245 PERCENT
——— RATE PER 100,000 INHABITANTS UP 204 PERCENT

CRIME INDEX TRENDS

(Percent change 1971 over 1970, offenses known to the police)

Population Group and Area	Number of Agencies	Population in thousands	Total	Violent	Property	Murder	Forcible Rape	Robbery	Aggravated Assault	Burglary	Larceny $50 and Over	Auto Theft
Total all agencies	5,619	165,157	+ 6	+ 9	+ 6	+10	+10	+10	+ 8	+ 8	+ 5	+ 2
Cities over 25,000	878	89,668	+ 5	+ 9	+ 4	+12	+ 9	+10	+ 7	+ 7	+ 2	+ 1
Suburban area	2,289	55,396	+11	+13	+11	+ 6	+ 9	+18	+11	+11	+13	+ 7
Rural area	1,289	20,550	+10	+ 8	+10	+ 3	+12	+19	+ 6	+10	+12	+ 3
Over 1,000,000	6	18,743	+ 3	+10	+ 1	+17	+10	+11	+ 5	+ 4	− 4	+ 2
500,000 to 1,000,000	20	12,965	− 3	...	− 3	+ 4	− 1	− 1	+ 2	.....	− 4	− 6
250,000 to 500,000	30	10,466	+ 7	+13	+ 6	+ 5	+20	+13	+13	.....	+ 2	+ 1
100,000 to 250,000	97	13,897	+ 6	+14	+ 6	+12	+17	+17	+10	+ 9	+ 4	+ 2
50,000 to 100,000	245	17,010	+10	+12	+10	+18	+13	+17	+ 8	+12	+ 9	+ 5
25,000 to 50,000	480	16,587	+10	+11	+10	+16	+ 6	+15	+ 8	+12	+ 9	+ 7
10,000 to 25,000	1,070	16,786	+12	+12	+12	+16	+11	+16	+10	+11	+14	+ 7
Under 10,000	2,054	10,265	+13	+11	+13	+30	+ 3	+23	+ 8	+14	+15	+ 6

CRIME INDEX TRENDS BY GEOGRAPHIC REGION
(1971 over 1970)

Region	Total	Violent	Property	Murder	Forcible Rape	Robbery	Aggravated Assault	Burglary	Larceny $50 and Over	Auto Theft
Northeastern States	+10	+19	+ 8	+20	+13	+24	+12	+11	+ 5	+ 7
North Central States	+ 3	+ 1	+ 3	+ 6	+ 8	...	+ 1	+ 7	+ 3	− 3
Southern States	+ 4	+ 6	+ 4	+ 7	+11	+ 1	+ 9	+ 5	+ 4	− 2
Western States	+ 8	+11	+ 8	+11	+ 7	+13	+ 9	+ 8	+10	+ 3

In years gone by, the rural dweller became a gun owner because of his physical isolation from any source of assistance. He defended his livestock from predators and added meat to his table with game. Although there is no accurate count of the nation's guns, it is estimated that those living in rural areas, less than 20 percent of the nation's population, possess 35 percent of the privately owned firearms. In the event of gun confiscation such as that proposed by the notorious Hart Bill of 1971, better than one out of every two farm families would have firearms to give up.

Based on the number of participants and the dollars spent for the activity, hunting is one of the nation's major sports. In 1971, nearly 23 million hunters were licensed. Well over half that number came from the rural areas and small towns of America. Again, *if guns are outlawed, the population group that will lose the most is the American farmer.*

If one murdered life could have been defended by a firearm, then there is no basis for confiscation or registration. At stake, however, is a moral issue more basic than that of one life or one thousand. By law, by amendment to the Constitution of the United States, the right to keep and bear arms shall not be infringed. The more than 20,000 gun laws and codes across the nation are in violation of the Constitution.

If those who infringe upon this right wish to persist, another amendment to the Constitution is required. Nothing less.

Perhaps then August 28 of 1963 in Apartment 3C at 57 East 88th Street need not be repeated. Two New York City roommates, Janice Wylie and Emily Hoffert, would not see the evening newscasts of the thousands of poor people who marched to the nation's capital on that hot day.

The hands of the electric clock in the room near Park Avenue that they shared were stopped forever at 10:37. The unplugged cord trailed senselessly across Emily's lips, spattered with blood from repeated stabbings.

An intruder had forced his way into the apartment. He bludgeoned one girl at a time and tied them together. Janice was disemboweled, while Emily's head and neck were stabbed again and again with knives from the kitchen drawer.

Newsweek had just lost a research assistant, and one New York suburb would never have the new teacher hired for that fall. Neither Janice nor Emily nor their third roommate, who was at work that day, qualified for handgun ownership under the Sullivan Law.

They were not two of several ghetto murders that occur each week in New York City. Apartment 3C is in the heart of Manhattan's fashionable East Side. The social status of their neighborhood no more protected the girls than did the isolation of the Clutter farmhouse from their nearest neighbor.

Like Nancy Clutter in Holcomb, Kansas, who was aware of an intruder in her family's house, Janice Wylie was unable to come to the defense of her roommate who was bludgeoned first.

By an unconstitutional law, there was no handgun in the apartment.